Countries

HELLO from SINGAPORE

C. Manica

Copyright © 2022 by C. Manica

All rights reserved.

No portion of this book may be reproduced in any form without written permission from the publisher or author, except as permitted by U.S. copyright law.

Hello, I'm Olivia Otter.
I'm going to tell you
about my country
Singapore!

So, where is Singapore?

Singapore is a small island country and city-state in South East Asia.

It's here! Can you see it?

I think we need a magnifying glass... There it is!

LET'S ZOOM IN!

Singapore is only around 730 km² (282 sq mi). It's very small, but modern and wealthy.

2

Here are some quick facts about Singapore!

Singapore is a parliamentary republic.

SINGAPORE PARLIAMENT HOUSE

We have a president, who is the head of state, and a prime minister, who is the head of government.

We celebrate our National Day on August 9.

Our currency is the Singapore dollar.

Our motto is "Majulah Singapura". It's Malay for "Onward Singapore". It's on our coat of arms, and it's also the title of our national anthem.

Our national flower is Vanda Miss Joaquim orchid.

The Merlion is our national mascot. It's a mythical creature with the head of a lion and the body of a fish.

4

Singapore has a tropical climate. It's always hot and humid there!

The average temperature is between 25 °C (77 °F) and 32 °C (89.6 °F).

There are no distinct seasons in Singapore, and it rains a lot throughout the year.

The month with the most rain is December, while the least is February.

There is a main island and 63 other smaller islands in Singapore. Most of the small islands are uninhabited.

Singapore has four official languages!

They are:
English, Malay, Mandarin, and Tamil.

That's because the main ethnic groups in Singapore are Chinese, Malay, and Indian.

There are also other ethnic groups called Eurasian and Peranakan.

The Eurasians are people of mixed European and Asian descent who have been living in the area since the 19th century.

The Peranakans or Strait Chinese are people whose ancestors came from China in the 15th century and married local Malay women.

TRADITIONAL PERANAKAN HOUSES

There are also people from all over the world living and working in Singapore.

So, of course you can find foods from many different countries, but you should try the local favorites!

The best place to get Singaporean food is at a "hawker center," an open-air food court with stalls selling delicious local dishes.

Kaya toast is a popular Singaporean breakfast.

Kaya is a sweet coconut milk custard spread. *Kaya* toast is usually eaten together with soft-boiled eggs.

 In Singapore, traditionally soft-boiled eggs are eaten not with a sprinkle of salt but with a squirt of dark soy sauce.

Roti prata is an Indian flatbread. It can be eaten plain or with fillings such as eggs or cheese and served with a small bowl of curry.

 *Chili crab* is Singapore's national dish. It's crabs cooked in a spicy, sweet, tangy, and savory sauce.

9

Nasi lemak is rice cooked in coconut milk, served with anchovies, peanuts, *sambal* (chili paste), and eggs, meat, or chicken.

Satays are grilled chicken, beef, or pork skewers, eaten with peanut sauce.

Noodles are very popular in Singapore. There are so many noodle dishes to try!

BAN MIAN

HOKKIEN MEE

LAKSA

HOR FUN

Hainanese chicken rice is another popular dish. It's simple but yummy!

Chendol is a dessert made with shaved ice, topped with coconut milk, *gula melaka* (palm sugar) syrup, red beans, and *chendol* (rice flour jelly).

Kueh tutu is a steamed rice flour cake filled with grated coconut or ground peanuts and *gula melaka*.

Have you tried Singaporean ice cream sandwich? It's a thick slab of ice cream wrapped in a slice of bread or served between two wafers.

It comes in a variety of flavors, from "normal" ones like chocolate and vanilla to more "exotic" ones such as sweet corn, red beans, purple yam, YUMMY and durian.

Do you know what durian is?

11

Durian* is a tropical fruit with a spiky shell and a strong smell, but a lot of people love its sweet, creamy taste.

Other tropical fruits you can find in Singapore are...

rambutan*

mangosteen

longan

jackfruit

starfruit

... and many more!

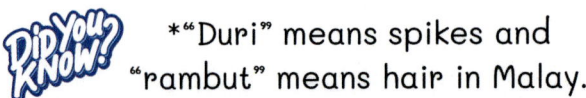

*"Duri" means spikes and "rambut" means hair in Malay.

Now, let's visit famous landmarks in Singapore!

You can see all of them in one day, because they are close together.

The Merlion sculpture at Merlion Park is probably Singapore's most famous landmark.

The nearby Esplanade-Theatres on the Bay is famous too! It's a center of performing arts. The locals call it the "durian" due to the building's spiky exterior.

From there, you can walk to Marina Bay Sands, another iconic landmark. It has a hotel, a shopping mall, restaurants, and an observation deck.

What is this unique building in front of Marina Bay Sands? This is the ArtScience Museum. It's shaped like a lotus flower.

The area in front of Marina Bay Sands/the ArtScience Museum is the perfect location to enjoy Singapore's skyline!

Across the road from Marina Bay Sands and the ArtScience Museum is Gardens by the Bay.

It's a large horticultural park famous for its giant glass dome greenhouses where you can find plants from all over the world.

The supertrees, massive tree-like structures in Gardens by The Bay, harvest solar energy and rainwater. They look cool too!

Even Singapore's airport is famous.

Changi airport is one of the best airports in the world. It's also one of the busiest!

There is an entertainment and shopping complex linked to the airport, called Jewel Changi, where you can see the world's tallest indoor waterfall, the Rain Vortex.

You can go shopping at Jewel Changi, but, Singapore's most iconic shopping district is Orchard Road. It's a 2.5 km (1.6 mi) stretch of shopping malls and hotels at the heart of Singapore.

While Orchard Road is Singapore's most iconic shopping district, Clarke Quay is Singapore's most iconic dining and entertainment district. It's located by the Singapore river.

Besides shopping, eating, and entertainment, Singapore also has a lot of museums and educational centers.

National Museum of Singapore is the country's oldest museum.

Here you can learn a lot about the history of Singapore, in a fun, interactive way.

If you like to have fun with science,
Science Centre Singapore is the place to be!

If you like animals, you can go to Singapore Zoo.

Singapore Zoo is an "open concept" zoo where the animals live in large enclosures resembling their natural habitats.

The zoo has a wildlife healthcare and research center. They support conservation projects in South East Asia. They also rescue and rehabilitate local wildlife.

If you'd rather spend time at the beach, Sentosa is the perfect place for you!

It's an island resort in the south of Singapore. It's connected to the main island by road, monorail, cable car, and pedestrian boardwalk.

SENTOSA BOARDWALK

SILOSO BEACH

There are three beaches in Sentosa; Siloso Beach, Palawan Beach, and Tanjong Beach. They all have calm water and fine sand.

Besides the beaches, Sentosa also has other attractions, such as S.E.A Aquarium, Universal Studios Singapore, and many, many more!

If you like nature, spending a day at the Botanic Gardens is a great idea.

Singapore Botanic Gardens was founded in 1859. It's huge! It covers 82 hectares (200 acres).

Jacob Ballas Children's Garden is a part of Singapore Botanic Gardens designed just for kids! You can play, explore, learn, and go on an adventure there.

There are a playground, a farm, an orchard, a forest with a stream and ponds, a waterfall, a suspension bridge, a hedge maze, and treehouses.

Singapore also has several nature reserves.

Bukit Timah Nature Reserve is the largest natural rainforest in Singapore.

Sungei Buloh Wetland Reserve is a sanctuary for native animals and migratory birds that use the area as a stopover.

Pulau Ubin is a small island located in the north-east of Singapore.

It's an island sanctuary for diverse plants and wildlife.

Singapore is home to many species of wildlife. You can find these animals in Singapore:

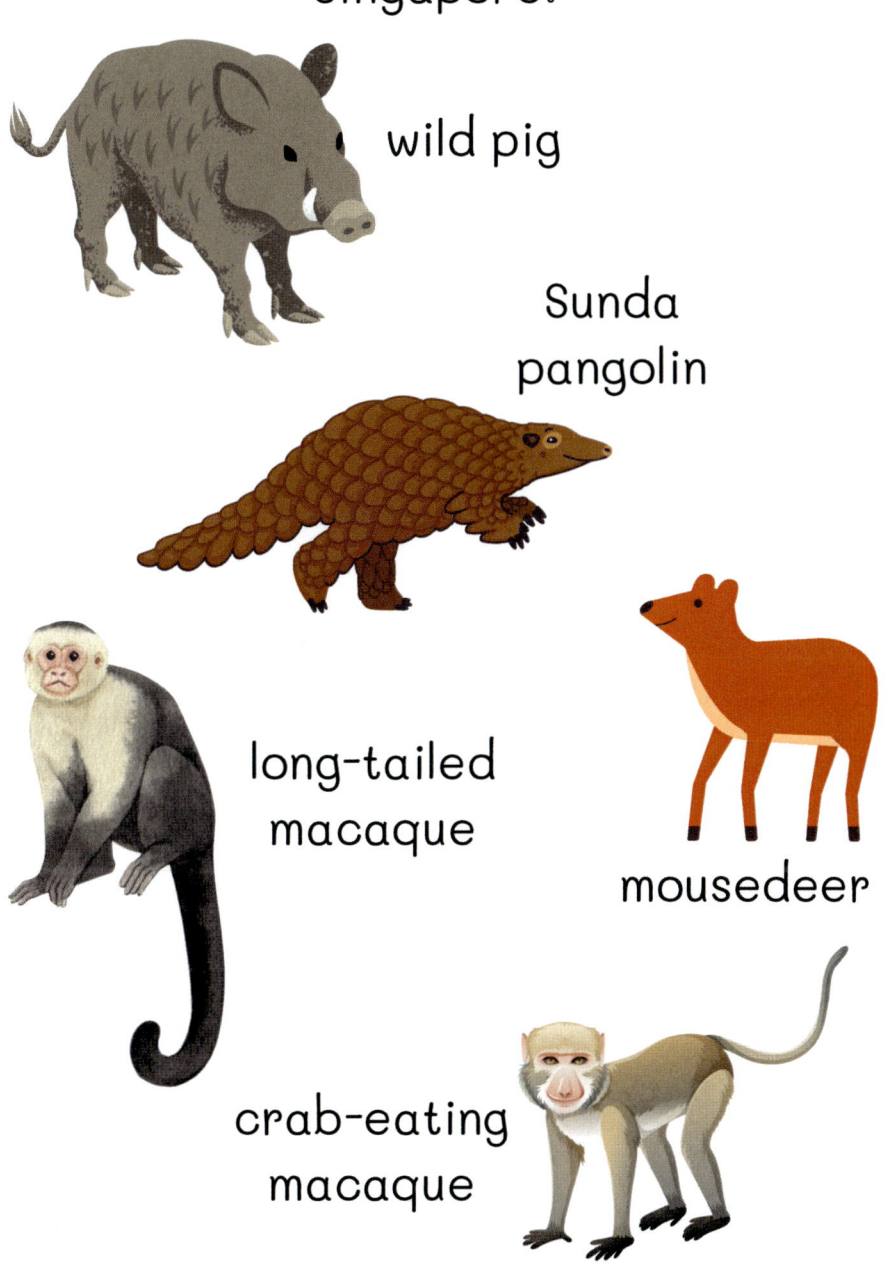

wild pig

Sunda pangolin

long-tailed macaque

mousedeer

crab-eating macaque

greater slow loris

hornbill

dugong

... and otters of course!

Wow, Singapore really has everything, right?
Would you like to come and visit me here? Where would you want to go in Singapore? What food would you want to try?

Bye... See you soon!

Collect all the books in the Countries for Kiddies series!

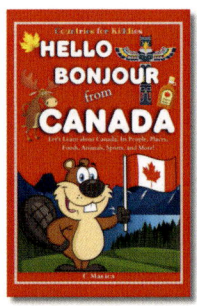 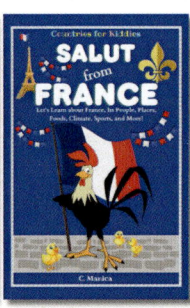   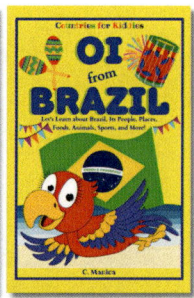

 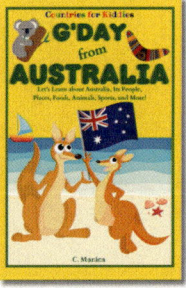 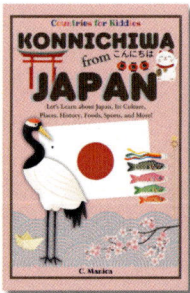  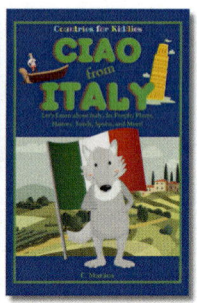

countries-for-kiddies.com

Made in the USA
Monee, IL
16 March 2025